From Worcestershire to North Wales in a Gig

A Parson's Journal
1835

From Worcestershire to North Wales in a Gig

A Parson's Journal
1835

Rev'd. Henry Charles Philpott M.A.

The journal of a holiday in North Wales in 1835 with additional notes on the route and on the Philpott family by Monica and John Heighes

IMAGES
PUBLISHING

Published in Great Britain 1994 by
Images Publishing (Malvern) Ltd.,
Upton-Upon Severn,
Worcestershire.

British Library Cataloguing in Publication Data

A catalogue record for this book is available
from the British Library

ISBN 1 897817 37 1

Designed and Produced by Images Publishing (Malvern) Ltd.
Printed and Bound in Great Britain by Bookcraft, Bath.

DEDICATION

The editor dedicates this book to her grandmother, Frances Burgess (née Philpott) 1851 – 1944, whose careful preservation of her father's journal allows us today to share the pre-Victorian tour of North Wales, undertaken by Henry Charles Philpott and his brother Thomas.

Acknowledgements

The contribution of the staff of Images Publishing and particularly that of Anita Hill and Chris Redman for drawings and book design is gratefully acknowledged.

The Rev'd Henry Charles Philpott M.A.

circa 1870

Rector of Earl's Croome 1855 to 1873

INTRODUCTION

On the 20th July 1835, Henry Charles Philpott, Curate of Severn Stoke in Worcestershire and his brother Thomas, Curate of Madresfield, near Malvern, set out from Madresfield with a pony and gig to holiday in North Wales. We know this because Henry kept a journal, in which he tells of the route, describes the scenery and comments on the state of the roads and the cleanliness or otherwise of the inns in which they stayed.

Severn Stoke is half way between Worcester and Tewkesbury, East of the Severn. Madresfield is a small village North East of Malvern. From Severn Stoke, it is likely that Henry crossed the Severn at Upton and then turned North through Hanley Castle to Madresfield, a distance of about 8 miles, to collect his brother.

The journal closes at Pedmore where their father was Rector, so the final paragraph of the journal concerning the excellence of the accommodation, refers to the family home, Pedmore Rectory. The journal has remained in the family, but its frank and honest revelations of the conditions experienced by the two brothers were considered to be of sufficient interest to offer it for wider reading.

It appears that the journal was started at the suggestion of Thomas, with the intention that the writing should be shared, but to Henry's annoyance and our good fortune, it was to Henry that the duty fell entirely. The journal has been preserved by his wife, his daughter, Frances, his grand-daughter and is now in the possession of his great grand-daughter.

The journey of Henry and Thomas was made in a gig;

this is a two wheeled vehicle pulled by a pony. It could accommodate two passengers sitting side by side facing forward and usually there was a compartment under the seat with rear facing doors, for a small amount of luggage.

The holiday of 1835 started with a visit to a third brother, Other, who was Curate of Clungunford, Shropshire. They then continued through Bishop's Castle to Welshpool, Dolgellau, (from where they climbed Cadair Idris), Barmouth, up the coast to Harlech, across to Llanberis, (from where they did not climb Snowdon), to return through Llangollen and Shrewsbury. Excluding local excursions, the journey from Madresfield to Pedmore was over 260 miles, this being spread over 11 days of travel during the 16 days of holiday, giving an average distance covered of 24 miles a day of travel.

The journal in the following pages has been transcribed as faithfully as possible, using Henry's punctuation and spelling. There are two words in the text which are not understood and are included as they appear to us, but in brackets followed by a question mark. There is also one sentence which is illegible.

The sections of the journal each start with a date in July or August. Our additional notes, made when following the route in 1992, are headed with place names.

Journal of a Tour

through part

of

North Wales.

in

1835

The Holiday Route of Henry Charles and Thomas in 1835

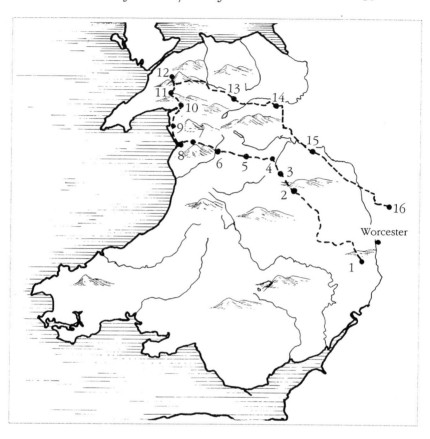

1. Madresfield, nr. Malvern	7. Dollgellau	12. Llanberis
2. Clungunford	8. Barmouth	13. Cernioge
3. Bishop's Castle	9. Harlech	14. Llangollen
4. Welshpool	10. Tan-y-bwlch	15. Shrewsbury
5. Cann Office Hotel	11. Beddgelert	16. Pedmore
6. Mallwyd		

On the 20th. July 1835, my brother Thomas & I set out from Madresfield to visit North Wales, & explore some of its beautiful scenery; & arrived at Clungunford Rectory at about half past six, we having ourselves fixed Other's dinner hour at six, that we might have plenty of time before us, & not keep him waiting; for the distance is 43 or 44 miles, & my little black mare uncommonly lazy, & Whipcord's persuasions have very little influence over her. Luckily, however, Other had not expected us sooner:- consequently had not been waiting dinner for us: &, consequently, the dinner was not spoiled:- till after we sat down - The next morning, notwithstanding all the pressing solicitations of our host to stay and partake of his hospitality another day, we resisted the temptation, & at 12 o'clock continued our travels.

Perhaps, had the accommodation for the inner and outer - mare been of a better description, we should have yielded, but with so long a journey before us, new hay and bad grooming seemed rather alarming. To be sure Davy Jones - though he says he will not yield to any man in handling a rake or a spade, - does not profess to set up for an accomplished groom; & if you had seen him spend 4 or 5 hours in the futile but arduous attempt to brush the mare clean, & the no less futile nor less arduous attempts to blow the dirt out of the curry comb; (the only expedient his brain could devise) and had listened to his repeated innocent exclamations - such as - 'Well, surelie there be a power o' dust in her' - and 'What a deal o' time it takes if every horse is made as clean as this 'n'

- etc. and had seen the mare when he had finished his labours - you would certainly have agreed with Davy Jones that he is not an accomplished groom.

It is about 12 miles from Clungunford to Bishop's Castle, & this we happily compleated in less than 2.½ hours! - but then I ought to add that some of the road is very bad, & a good deal of it hilly. Bishop's Castle has been described as a 'small but neat town'; - small it may be:- neat it is not: & I suspect the description to have been written by the celebrated learned pig - here, at least, is a numerous colony of that interesting quadruped, (who roam about unrestrained by those tyrannical prison & (clept?) stys & surely no other animal could consider Bishop's Castle neat. The vulgar saying - I will do so & so, -'please the pigs' must have had its origin at this place:- for here - their ease and convenience & pleasure seem to be chiefly consulted: & moreover, nothing *but the pigs could possibly be pleased here.*

From hence to Welsh Pool, through a well wooded & picturesque district, is about 15 miles, & so hilly, that tho' we left B.Castle before 4, we did not reach WPool until 20 minutes after 8 o'clock. After refreshing ourselves with tea and mutton chops (tea & dinner in one) I exercised my mind & my hand by writing the foregoing commencement of our journal which Thomas is to continue tomorrow night.

The Royal Oak Hotel, Welshpool.

MADRESFIELD TO CLUNGUNFORD AND WELSHPOOL

Thomas was Curate of Madresfield from 1823 – 1857. It would seem that he first served under the Rev'd. Reginald

Pindar, who was Rector from 1793 to 1832. He was succeeded by his son-in-law, Charles Hill who was Rector until he died in 1856. However, as Charles Hill was also Rector of Bromsberrow, some 10 miles from Madresfield, it would seem that Thomas had charge of the parish until the arrival of George Munn in 1856.

Thomas was also Perpetual Curate of the adjacent parish of Newland from 1831 to 1856. The term was used originally for a priest nominated by a lay Rector but in the 19th century, the title was used for the priest of a newly established parish. (see 'The Concise Oxford Dictionary of the Christian Church', published by Oxford University Press)

No record of the time Thomas spent in Madresfield was found in the church and he gets no mention in the church guide which seems sad after 34 years of service to the parish. But then, he was not Rector, even if the Rector did not live in the parish.

Adjacent to the church at Clungunford is Glebe Cottage, once the Rectory; some 100 metres from the church is a Victorian Rectory built in 1895 and now turned into flats and between this building and the church yard is a modern Rectory. The Rector was kind enough to produce a history of the parish and this recorded that there had been yet another Rectory which stood between the site of the present Rectory and the site of the Victorian one, but no longer exists. It was almost certainly this Rectory in which Henry and Thomas spent the first night of their holiday.

The church they would have seen was somewhat different, it having been restored in 1895, when the very solid tower was added. Perhaps on that morning in July

1835, the three clergy brothers strolled across to the church to share Morning Prayer, probably on one of the very rare occasions when all three were together as clerics. The church contains no record of Other's time at Clungunford.

Bishop's Castle is now by-passed by the A488. Pigs no longer roam the streets and the town may now be described as "small and neat". A small cattle market shows it to be the centre of a farming community.

July 22nd

Thomas behaves very shabbily – he refuses to perform his share of journal writing – a task I undertook only at his urgent request – so having begun it, I suppose the rest, as the old advertisements used to state, 'will be done by the same hand!' At about 10 o'clock this morning, after a stroll though the uninteresting town of Welsh Pool, we left the Royal Oak, a middling inn, (and where Thomas had more bedfellows than he found agreeable) but the best of the 20 and odd provided by the hospitable inhabitants for the refreshment of way worn travellers.

We saw this town to unusual advantage for the streets this morning were actually swept, & the houses cleansed (in consequence of a recommendation by the town cryer to that effect) to grace the entry of the Judge. The distance from hence to Can Office is about 15 miles – the first half of which (to Llanfair) presents some beautiful scenery – bold hills, covered with very luxuriant plantations, & at the bottom of the valley, the small river Vyrnevy, murmers over the obstructing rocks.

Can Office Hotel, Llangadfan.

At Can Office, a very dirty room, a dreadfully stinking table cloth and abominably filthy knives and forks & spoons, did not entirely destroy our appetites. How hungry we must have been! for we resisted the natural effects of this villainous & odoriferous combination – and dined! – In the afternoon we proceeded to Mallwyd, about 11 miles men & steed sadly tired by a most hilly and tedious road. When the new one is completed, this stage will be a much more agreeable one. Mallwyd is a small village with a tolerably comfortable inn (after Can Office, a princely one) situated near some fine mountain scenery.

Very near the inn is a small waterfall on the river Dovey, & a pretty rustic bridge. The church is remarkable for the situation of the Altar, which stands nearly in the midst of the chancel, which having been extended to the eastward by a Dr. Davies in the time of Archbishop Laud, he steadily refused, (in spite of the Archbishop's injunction to place the altar at the east end) to remove it from its original position. The church yard contains some beautiful yew trees – one of the largest we ever saw. A singular anecdote attaches to a very flourishing young one. Some years ago this tree was stolen, & after a lapse of 5 years it was discovered in a churchyard 20 miles off, claimed & restored to its native soil. This I repeat on the authority of the clerk, who mentioned the name of the place whence it was recovered, & seems an intelligent man.

Mallwyd church.

The Brigand's Hotel, Mallwyd.

WELSHPOOL TO MALLWYD

The Royal Oak Hotel is in the centre of Welshpool and still offers accommodation and refreshment to the traveller as well as to the local, as was apparent from the cheerful banter in the bar on the Saturday of our visit. It boasts only two stars by both A.A. and R.A.C. rating but the ground floor gave the impression of being worth more. The brochure shows it to have been run by the same family since 1927. If the spotless toilets are an indication of the running of the rest of the hotel, as they probably are, the brothers Philpott would have nothing to complain of here today.

We had been unable to locate the next port of call, Can

Office, on a map but enquiry at the Royal Oak revealed this also to be an hotel. The road from Welshpool follows the River Banwy and the Cann Office Hotel is on the outskirts of the village of Llangadfan. The hotel provides a leaflet with an interesting explanation of the name, well supported by documentation. The hotel is built on the site of a motte and bailey castle and papers in the National Library of Wales show that the inn sign was three cannes, (presumably drinking mugs or tankards) and the building was known as Tyn-y-ydomen, the house in the bailey. The term 'Office' is due to the setting up of a communications system by horse, and horses were kept at intervals to facilitate regular changes by the rider at 'posts' which were often situated at inns. There is a record that the inn at Tynydomen with the sign of the Three Canns was used as a post office in 1677. Hence the name, Cann Office.

The road to Mallwyd is still hilly. The route of the old road is not obvious today although the O.S. map indicates that it may have crossed the river further east than does the present road. That the brothers found the road tedious could not have been due to the scenery but was more likely to have been because of the frequent hill climbs which caused them to descend from the gig and walk. The scenery here certainly begins to offer a taste of what is to come between Mallwyd and Dolgellau.

The inn at Mallwyd is called 'The Brigands Hotel' and today it is a centre for fishing and walking. It stands at the junction of the A458 from Welshpool and the A489 from Machynlleth. Mallwyd is still a small village. The church is worth a visit. Today, the altar is in the conventional position in the chancel which has a pleasing barrel roof. The Dr. John Davies who is reported in the journal to have refused to move the altar, was John Davies D.D., Rector from 1604 to 1634 and who assisted with the Revised Translation of the Bible of 1620. He is buried on the south side of the chancel and the inscription reads:

MAN BEDD
Y Dr. JOHN DAVIES
O FALLWYD
1567 – 1644

July 23rd

Detained the whole of this morning at Mallwyd by a steady rain. After an early dinner proceeded to Dollgelly – about 12 miles – through some fine mountain scenery.

HOTELS VISITED		WATERFALLS	
1.	The Brigand's Hotel – Mallwyd	8.	Pystyl Cain
2.	Dolgellau (hotel identity uncertain)	9.	Rhaiadyr y Mawddach
		10.	Rhaiadyr du
3.	Tyn-y-groes Hotel – Ganllwyd	11.	The Waterfalls at Festiniog
4.	The Lion Hotel – Barmouth		
5.	The Castle Hotel (background view of Harlech Castle)	MOUNTAINS	
6.	The Oakley Arms – Tan-y-bwlch	12.	Cadair Idris
7.	The Dolbadarn Hotel – Llanberis	13.	Snowdon

The Holiday Route

"Some fine mountain scenery" between Mallwyd and Dolgellau.

The evening was beautiful, & the air unusually clear; & Cader Idris, ever changing its shape & aspect, towered above the surrounding, yet still lofty, mountains. Emerging from this grand & rugged scene, the first view of Dolgelly, & the prettily wooded vale in which it is situated strikes you as peculiarly calm & pleasing; an impression much heightened by the sudden contrast. We arrived here about 7 o'clock, & to our annoyance & disappointment, found we might each of us exclaim with Titus (at least if we had any friends to exclaim to) – "Amici! diem perdidi"* – for at Dolgelly there had been no rain – It had fallen so thickly & without

---

* Amici! diem perdidi – Friends, I have wasted a day

intermission, that we never suspected that it might have been partial.

July 24th

After a pleasant saunter through some of the beautiful country surrounding the town, we drove to visit the celebrated waterfalls on the Tan y Bwlch road. Leaving our gig at the Traveller's Rest – a small wayside inn, about 4½ miles from Dolgelly, we took a guide – a shrewd intelligent, stunted urchin – whose native place, as he told us, was 'the little country about Tan y Bwlch (an expression which quite puzzles us) – & walked to the three falls. The first, Rhaiadyr Du (the black Cataract) though disappointing us as a waterfall – the season being very dry – presents an imposing aspect from the immenseness of the dark rock down which the water foams, & the ponderous broken masses forming for a considerable distance the channel of ye. stream.

The Tyn-y-groes Hotel on the way to "the celebrated waterfalls on the Tan-y-bwlch road".

25

Henry's great grand-daughter at the falls in 1992 – 157 years after her great grandfather.

From hence to the next falls Rhaiadyr y Mawddach, is about 3 miles – some of it very rough walking; & the day proving very hot, & we – not proving quite first rate pedestrian tourists, were a good deal tired; but our toil was amply recompensed by this beautiful cataract, & its rival neighbour – Pisyyll y Cayne (or spout of the Cayne) I am in doubt to which of these two to award a preference; & it would be certainly a great piece of presumption in me to speak decisively. Thos. (I think), admires the first most, while I upon the whole incline to the latter. The approach through a narrow pass, along a shelving ledge between hanging rocks, & the wild, & romantic & dark scenery surrounding the first, are its peculiar features:- of the latter, the volume of water is greater & more unbroken; falling from a great height into a calm, circular, capacious, basin; & the adjacent scenery is altogether of a more peaceful character. To obtain a better view, I crossed to the opposite side by the help of the fragments of broken rock which form the outer edge of the basin; & was some time before I could muster sufficient resolution to retrace my adventurous steps – this however, at length, I accomplished in safety.

Mallwyd to Dolgellau

Henry gives this part of the journey just four words, 'some fine mountain scenery' and later describes the Vale of Ffestiniog more enthusiastically. The scenery before starting the descent into Dolgellau must rate as some of the finest in North Wales. On the day of our visit, we also experienced heavy rain and almost vertical streams were cascading down the mountainside. Here perhaps, Henry was a little economic in his praise of the North Wales scenery.

The Dolgellau Area Record Office, a part of the Gwynedd County Council County Archive Department, could not trace which inns were likely to have been in existence in 1835. However, they did find a reference to guided tours to Cadair Idris by horseback, which started from an inn which stood just below the present Council offices, but no longer exists. It is possible that Henry and Thomas chose the Golden Lion in which to stay, which does still exist and was once a coaching inn with stables.

Dolgellau is a pleasant town to explore. The information Office in the middle of the town, offers a map of the town and a suggested trail in order to find the places of interest.

THE CELEBRATED WATERFALLS

To describe the road north from Dolgellau today as the Tan-y-bwlch road would be unusual. It needed the Landranger Series O.S. map to find Tan-y-bwlch marked in less significant print than nearby Maentwrog. Today the road is the A470(T) signed Ffestiniog and Betws-y-coed and it is the left hand fork of the A487, north of Lake Trawsfynidd which leads to Tan-y-bwlch.

Some 4½ miles out of Dolgellau, just before the village of Ganllwyd is the Tyn-y-groes Hotel. The proprietor had no knowledge of the hotel ever having been called The Traveller's Rest, (Tyn-y-groes means 'The house at the crossroads', we were told) but as it is 400 years old and the right distance from Dolgellau, this is almost certainly the inn where pony and gig were left for the walk to 'the celebrated waterfalls on the Tan-y-bwlch road'.

There is no need in the idle 20th century to walk from the Tan-y-groes Hotel, (although the very welcoming proprietors would make a visit worthwhile). The Forestry Commission has constructed roads throughout the area know as Coed-y-brenin. The falls are reached by forking right at the end of the village of Ganllwyd, then cross the bridge and immediately fork right. However, before doing so, a short distance further up the A470 is the Forestry Commission Visitor Centre and information collected there before visiting the falls is recommended.

A car may be parked at the first wooden bridge and as there are bridges across the two rivers which join below the falls, it is possible to walk up one side of the river and back down the other – a round trip of three to four miles. This reduces very considerably the walk made by the brothers.

From Henry's description of the falls, little appears to have changed. However, since the 1835 visit, an industry has come and gone. In 1840, gold mines were opened up in the vicinity of the falls and disused buildings with a mill race and sluice mechanism, (but no sluice gate), remain as evidence of the use of water power to crush the ore to extract the gold. The crushing mechanism rescued from the building and restored, can be seen at the Visitor Centre. On the day of our visit, a man was seen panning for gold in the shallows of the river.

July 25th

Rose early this morning in order that we might attain the summit of Cader Idris whilst the atmosphere was still clear. Our guide, Richard Pugh, provided horses, & accompanied us on foot, & after two hours toil we reached the top, & were fortunate in having the atmosphere unusually clear. The scenery from this lofty spot is not very varied, but consists of scarcely anything more than a wavy view of mountain beyond mountain, except on the Barmouth side where you have a view of the sea. What best repays the labour of ascending is a mountain lake, not far off, to which the guide took us – remarkable for its depth, & for the grand and rocky mountain on one side, which rises perpendicularly from the shore, the varied hues of which are peculiarly fine and rich. It has, I believe, been painted by Wilson.

We remained about an hour on the summit – & at the lake – & regained our inn about 5 hours after we had left it; our tough old guide, tho' upwards of 60 winters had passed over his head & he had ridden eighty miles on the previous day – the freshest of the party – horses included. After an early dinner we left Dolgelly & proceeded to Barmouth, a distance of about 10 miles, & highly enjoyed that much-to-be-admired & very beautiful drive.

Barmouth July 27th

We passed a quiet Sunday here & went twice to church – or rather Chapel of ease, for Barmouth is not a parish. There are usually during the summer months four services here, two in Welsh, & two in English.

St. David's church, Barmouth, built in 1830, the Chapel of Ease.

After morning service we took rather a long stroll on the sands which, when the tide is out, are very extensive, & were both much tired; and the weather being uncommonly hot, rose this morning feverish and good for nothing. Took a quiet drive after breakfast towards Dolgelly, a road that will never tire even the coldest admirers of beautiful scenery –

woods, water, & mountains being most harmoniously blended: found the heat of the sun quite overpowering.

The Painting of The Ferry House and Mawddach estuary by G.R. Clarke, the Upton-on-Severn architect and brother of Henry Charles' son-in-law.

After dinner took a longer ramble than we intended over the rocky mountains which rise abruptly at the back of the town, & had nearly lost our way, but were repayed for our exertions. Were it not for the vile, abominable sand banks, which rise immediately before the houses, & shut out the sea, & were there a better conducted Inn, Barmouth might be a pleasant little bathing place at which to sojourn at – but with the present state of things, – we were disappointed & disgusted. There are lodging houses which are no doubt preferable in accommodation as they certainly are in situation, – but you cannot get rid of the sand banks.

DOLGELLAU TO BARMOUTH

It is not surprising that with time to spare, Henry and Thomas chose to drive back along the road to Dolgellau to enjoy the scenery of the Mawddach estuary once again.

The name of the inn in which they stayed in Barmouth is not given; That the journal states, 'were there a better conducted inn . . .' suggests that they had no choice. However, the present proprietor of The Lion told us that her hotel was built in the 17th century and a book by Ann Rhydderch published by Gwynedd Archives Service reprints from 'The Cambrian Tourist or Post-Chaise Companion Through Wales' of 1821, which indicates that the Cors-y-gedol, now closed, would also have been available.

The Lion Hotel, Barmouth.

34

The Chapel of Ease, to which they twice went during their Sunday in Barmouth, is St. David's, a cruciform church overlooking the harbour which was built in 1830 and is a part of the parish of Llanaber with Barmouth. It is still in use and beautifully kept.

In 1835, Barmouth must have been a small town clustered round the harbour, dependant on fishing, some ship building and the summer visitors and beginning to extend towards Harlech, although Ann Rhydderch states that in the mid eighteenth century, Barmouth was the main port of Merionethshire, taking advantage of the Merioneth wool trade. The sea came up to what is now the main street as mooring rings were found in the rock at the Lion Hotel. (The sea is know to have receded from Harlech in a similar manner) The town has extended west to an extensive sea front beyond the railway which came in 1867. By 1895, it had become necessary to build the present parish church, St. John the Evangelist, to accommodate the expanding population.

Harlech. July 28th.

Left Barmouth this morning at 7 o'clock – not grieved to make our escape:- had a cool and pleasant ride to Harlech – 10 miles – the greater part of which is flat and uninteresting; until indeed you approach Harlech, & the Castle, the situation of which is very imposing. The Inn, which is close to the Castle is a quiet & comfortable one, & what made it still more interesting to us, we had an excellent breakfast placed before us, made more tempting by cleanliness, a virtue which we have sighed for, a virtue which we well know how to appreciate, a virtue which we are ready to place at least next after the four cardinal ones.

Harlech is still a beautiful spot, & must have been eminently so when the sea washed the foot of the rock on which the Castle is built, but it has receded at least a mile. From the window of our room, upstairs, we had a fine open view of Cardigan Bay: & Thomas was tempted by the appearance of the shore, & a new bathing machine, only finished yesterday, & entirely a novel introduction here, to go down & have a dip in the ocean, but the tide being out, found the water very shallow; & the walk much longer than it appears to the eye.

The view across the golf course from Harlech Castle.

The Castle Hotel, Harlech, from the castle.

We truly regretted that we had not sooner known the beauty and accommodation of this place, as in that case, we should certainly have left Barmouth yesterday, & spent a whole day here. Harlech was once a town of some importance, but has now dwindled down to a mere Welsh village. We went over the Castle – a small, but remarkably strong fortress – accessable only on one side, & celebrated as being the last Castle in Wales that yielded to the parliamentary forces during the rebellion against Charles ye. first.

The (hiatrup?) & attention of the people of the Inn induced us to stay & take an early dinner; & we were not disappointed: for we sat down to the best dinner we have eaten, since we left Clungunford. Fresh Turbot & Soles (tho' it was almost a sin to catch the little things) & a capital roast duck & green peas, afforded us a meal that might have satisfied epicures even. In the afternoon we drove to Tan y Bwlch by a new road through a strikingly picturesque & mountainous district; the most beautiful part of which is where you arrive at an arm of the sea, which at high water has every resemblance of a very fine lake with richly wooded hills rising on all sides from its shores.

The road itself must not be left unnoticed, being so well managed, (tho' the whole country is so very precipitous) as to be almost on a level the whole ten miles. Nothing appears to me so difficult in writing, as to convey anything like a correct notion of scenery; my undertaking therefore is a very hopeless one, where almost every mile presents a scene equally worthy of description as the preceding.

The arm of the sea which Henry thought resembled a lake.

All that I can do is to vary the terms a little – accordingly some places are beautiful, some picturesque, others – bold – romantic – lovely – grand – enchanting etc. etc. This is meant as an apology for the very meagre & unsatisfactory notice of Tan y Bwlch which follows.

It is, I think in some respects as enchanting in situation as any place we have yet seen during our tour. It is not so bold & mountainous as some views we have met with – not so sequestered as others – & has not the advantage of the sea: – but then it can boast of very varied ground – precipitous rocks, green sloping woods & smiling vallies. Mr Oakley has a very pretty place, close to the inn – which we visited. Rhododendrons flourish here amazingly. We saw one which *measured 50 yards round. This is fact altho' some persons may perhaps think it is nothing but a flourish.*

The magnificent rhododendrons at Plas Tan-y-bwlch.

BARMOUTH TO TAN-Y-BWLCH

The road from Barmouth to Harlech is certainly flat once it has climbed up out of Barmouth but it is hardly uninteresting, with the sea and surf swept sandy beaches on one side and the mountains rising up on the other beyond the coastal plain.

Today, the number of small villages which dot the route, consist of a mixture of older houses and modern bungalows, popular with people retiring from England. The church we attended on our Sunday in the area specifically advertised its only service of the day as being in English.

A number of large permanent caravan sites can be seen

from the road, but there are long stretches of coastline still looking very natural. We were told however, that coastal development at Barmouth is the cause of pebbles beginning to be found along the sandy beaches.

The narrow and winding streets of Harlech are bypassed by the main road which runs under the castle on the seaward side where ships once unloaded supplies for the castle. As Henry and Thomas found, the distance to the sea is deceptive and today there is room for the 18 hole Royal St. David's golf course between the castle and the sea. Measurement on the O.S. map shows the distance to be about 0.6 miles.

The imposing castle can still be visited; the bases of the drawbridge towers can be seen adjacent to the entrance steps but otherwise the walls are substantially intact. An exhibition illustrates the history of the castle and a model shows what it probably looked like when it was in use to defend that part of the country. For the agile, it is possible to climb to the top of one of the turrets and a walk round the terracing brings to the imagination the thought of members of the small garrison patrolling the walls on the lookout for any approach from the sea.

The inn where Henry and Thomas enjoyed breakfast and later, dinner before continuing to Tan-y-bwlch, must have been the Castle Hotel, immediately behind the castle.

The road, as Henry states, is level to Tan-y-bwlch, except for the gentle decline from Harlech until three miles further on, it rejoins the A496 coastal road. The 'arm of the sea which, at high water has every resemblance of a very fine lake . . .' is the estuary of the Afon Dwyrd which flows through the Vale of Ffestiniog.

July 29th.

Slept well in comfortable beds, & after breakfast, drove in our gig, through the vale of Maentwrog to see the waterfalls at Festiniog, by which name the valley is also called. We did not discover the one above the bridge, but found the others well worth our labour. But the vale itself is the object of the greatest interest, & from the hills around Festiniog you take in the whole of it in one view. Having now become better aquainted with this beautiful valley, I have no inclination to retract my epithet of enchanting which I used last night, but pronounce it as displaying unquestionably the most lovely scenery we have met with in the whole of North Wales. [The next sentence has been written over and is not clear but appears to continue in praise of the scenery] Everything indeed is here to render this spot pre-eminent. The vale itself is chamingly green, and rich, and fresh looking, being fertilized by a pretty little river which wanders through its whole length; while, on each side of the Vale, arise rocks and mountains of entirely different hues & characters. Some are entirely covered with woods, some with bright purple heath, others again, & in general the loftiest, are totally bare & rugged – all adding their own peculiar features & beauties to the whole, & combining to render this never-to-be-forgotten scene beautiful exceedingly. Having taken our gig back to the inn, we walked two or three miles to see some more falls beyond the pretty little village of Maintwrog. The sun was scorching; & some part of our path being very steep,

Thomas, who is far from stout, visited one only of the falls – there are two – & unfortunately, that which is least worth seeing. He walked back to the road, quietly, whilst my guide, a little fellow of six years old, unacquainted with English, preceded me to the Rhaiadyr Du. Arrived there and much regretted that Thomas had not accompanied me – for this waterfall is uncommonly grand, & the two points from which it is seen to the greatest advantage, almost equally terrific. The water has nothing to obstruct its course, but the entire stream of the river, undivided, comes thundering down one, immense, perpendicular mass of rock into the dark basin below. Here everything is of the most sombre character – dark hanging foliage – black rocks – blacker water – & with such a scene all around & below you – standing on a little jutting rock, perhaps a yard square – it makes you feel queer, & quake, to look down (I should suppose 2 or 3 hundred feet) & see only empty space between you and the foaming channel of the stream.

The other point, a little lower down, has much of the same character, only that the course of the stream below the fall is more distinctly seen. Having joined Thomas again, I took off my boots and stockings & taking him on my back, forded ye. river, to avoid a mile or two of hot dusty road. Gained our Inn heated, & tired & hungry: & having dressed ourselves, heartily enjoyed a very good dinner.

At Tan-y-bwlch

The inn at Tan-y-bwlch was the Oakley Arms, which on the day of our visit, appeared to be closed. It is built of dark grey stone, which makes it look cold and gaunt, particularly without the activity which must have surrounded it in the days of horse travel. It stands on the A487 Porthmadog to Ffestiniog road across the river from 'the pretty little village of Maintwrog', which is still a pretty little village today, with the village post office doubling as an information centre.

The Oakley Arms is opposite the gate of Plas Tan-y-bwlch, the estate of the Oakley family in which was found the amazing rhododendrons, which can still be seen below the terrace of the house. The estate came into the Oakley family through the female line of the Evans of Tan-y-bwlch and the Griffiths or Gruffyd family of Bachsaint, near Cricieth, the Oakleys originating from Staffordshire.

The Oakley Arms, Tan-y-bwlch.

As William Griffiths Oakley is reported to have extended the front of the Oakley Arms and as he died in 1835, it seems likely that the hotel today looks much as it did when the brothers stayed there. Plas Tan-y-bwlch today is owned by the County Council and is used as a residential study centre for Snowdonia, with a quite extensive range of courses on offer throughout the year. Anyone lucky enough to find the Manager of the Centre with a few minutes to spare will be well rewarded, if they are interested in the house and its history.

From the church at Ffestiniog there is a beautiful view of the Vale and just below the church, on the road back to Maintwrog, is a gate with the first of many signs to Rhaedr Cynfal. The path should not be attempted after rain without

45

boots, but otherwise, it is moderately easy walking for about a mile to see from above, an awesome plunge of water into the gorge below. It is not clear however, if this was visited by Henry and Thomas as the journal talks of 'waterfalls'. It is possible therefore that they did not reach Ffestiniog but found the falls on the Afon Goedol which can be reached west of the road to Blaenau Ffestiniog a road which did not exist in 1835.

The falls beyond the village of Maintwrog can be reached from a lane which climbs up behind (on the village side of) a small hydro electric power station.

The falls beyond Maintwrog.

It would seem from his description however, that Henry climbed up on the other side of the river.

It must have been the bridge by the power station at which Thomas waited for Henry's return – quite a long wait as the falls are a considerable distance from the road. It says something for Henry's stamina that after the second such walk and climb on a hot day, he could still find the energy to carry Thomas on his back to ford the river. The river they forded can be seen meandering through the meadows from the terrace of Plas Tan-y-bwlch.

July 30th.

After an early breakfast, left Tan y Bwlch & its comfortable inn for Llanberis in order to see the singular valley called the Pass of Llanberis & with the intention of ascending Snowdon. It is ten miles from Tan y Bwlch to Bedgelert, the former part of the road very hilly, & almost all of it very beautiful – more particularly – Pont Aberglasslynn, where there is just room for the road and the river between lofty & inaccessible rocks. The view from the bridge is exceedingly fine both ways, but more especially looking up the steam, through these rocky mountains. Baited at Bedgelert, & then commenced the very toilsome stage to Llanberis – 12 miles – of this we were obliged to walk a considerable portion, & even then the mare seemed to find it hard work to draw the empty gig. The new road is unfortunately not yet finished, but it will be a great relief to travellers.

The Afon Glaslyn near Beddgelert, the view from the bridge which Henry thought "exceedingly fine".

48

This bad road terminates at the junction with the Capel Curig & Llanberis road, an excellent one & which has been opened about four years on which is the Pass, which we were not aware of, until we arrived at it, when we exclaimed "This must be the Pass of Llanberis"! It is indeed extremely grand, & imposing.

Excepting the road itself, and some rude attempts at stone walls, probably marking the division of property, there is nothing to indicate the labours, or the existence of man: – but the scene of desolate grandeur is complete. Rough, craggy rocks towering on each side you up to the skies – & at the bottom of the narrow valley innumerable ponderous fragments thickly scattered in all directions, as if two contending armies of giants on the opposite heights had torn them from their native rocks to use as deadly missiles. But to give an adequate description of this scene requires the eye of an artist, & the pen of a poet.

We were peculiarly fortunate in having uncommonly clear weather; for these mountains are frequently enveloped in mists or clouds for many days together. With respect to the very extensive prospect from the top of Snowdon, the reader (should I happen to have one) will I hope excuse my making any particular observations, for this sole & simple reason – I did not ascend it – My short excursion through N. Wales has fully convinced me that in a mountainous district the finest scenery is not to be sought on the highest ground, but you must explore the vallies & the rivers. From the summit of the highest mountain you gain an extensive view, indeed, but you gain it at the expense of making all the other mountains around you look very small. You are told that from the top of Snowdon you can see, on a clear day, Ireland, Scotland, & England – the Isles of Man & Anglesea etc. Why you may see much farther than this, & a more sublime view too, any star-light night, without any climbing at all! And then, of course you are to lift up your hands & eyes and exclaim with Dominic Sampson, 'Prodigious'! To my mind Aeneas' map of wine spilt on the table – 'Hac ibat Simois, hic est Sigeia tellus' – was quite as edifying, & interesting.

We slept at the New Inn at Llanberis (quite a noble one) where we were not so comfortable as we should have been, had the house been less full. As it was, we were *obliged to occupy the Coffee-room in common with other parties, an arrangement which we, who are unaccustomed to much travelling, pronounced an abominable bore.*

The Dolbadarn Hotel, Llanberis.

TAN Y BWLCH TO LLANBERIS

It is likely that the route from Tan-y-bwlch was through Rhyd to Garreg before turning north on what is now the A4085 which joins the A498 at Porthmadog. The bridge from which Henry and Thomas were overawed by the Afon Glaslyn is where these two roads once again go their separate ways, the A4085 to Caernarfon and the A498 follows the river into Beddgelert. From Beddgelert, this road climbs steadily on the south side of Snowdon until it joins the Llanberis – Capel Curig road at the Gwryd Hotel.

The road which Henry and Thomas found so tiring before the construction of the new road, can be seen following the floor of the valley, at the end of which, it must have climbed very steeply. The New Inn is not known in Llanberis. The present Dolbadarn Hotel was built in 1802 and as it is unlikely that a small village would have two inns, it is probable that it is this one which in 1835, was still known as, 'the new inn'. It was originally a coaching inn and still maintains its tradition with horses by offering trecking over the lower slopes of Snowdon.

The old road from Beddgelert following the floor of the valley.

There were extensive slate workings east of Llanberis and the slate was brought from the quarry to the fascinating plant on the outskirts of the village which is now an industrial museum, the Welsh Slate Museum. The Museum of the North, a part of the National Museum of Wales, stands beside the main road, with plenty of parking space. It is also used by the National Grid Company for the start of tours to the Dinorwig pumped storage generation scheme. This is the electricity equivalent of a gas holder. When the electricity grid system is on light load, with power generation capacity to spare, power is used to drive pumps which lift water from the lower reservoir, Llyn Peris, at the side of the main road, to the upper reservoir, where it is held as potential energy for periods of high load, being able to contribute 1320 megawatts within 10 seconds.

Today, there is much to see in Llanberis besides Snowdon.

Cernioge July 31st

After breakfast left Llanberis, & drove to Capel Curig – 10 miles – stayed there only to bait; and proceeded to this place – 14½ miles – I have now an additional reason to rejoice that we gave up the ascent of Snowdon – for Thomas, who has not been by any means 'compos' corporis for some time, is materially indisposed this evening, & would probably have felt the fatigue very seriously. He could eat no dinner, but has taken a few mouthfuls of gruel, & is gone to bed.

LLANBERIS TO CERNIOGE

It may have been the developing illness of Thomas which resulted in the next part of the journey being accomplished with no sight seeing – the journal contains no mention of Betws-y-coed or the Swallow Falls. Capel Curig is at the junction with the A5.

Cernioge was difficult to find and we passed it twice before being told at Pentrefoelas Post Office that we should not be looking for a village or an inn but for a farm. Cernioge Mawr is very much a working farm today; the farmer was working hard well after 5.0 pm to brush out his cowshed but he paused in his work to confirm that the farmhouse was once the coaching inn, although today it is reduced in size, a part of it having been pulled down in the 1950's. The farmhouse lies well back from the road but close to the A5 on the opposite side of the road, is the stable building where Henry's mare would have been fed, (baited), watered and rested.

The Coaching stables at Cernioge.

Augt 1st

Altho' he slept well, Thomas is very feverish, & feels a good deal of pain & swallowed with great difficulty a small cup of cocoa for breakfast, prepared by the Landlady, Mrs Weaver, who has been very attentive, & anxious to do for him all in her power. We arrived at Corwen – 13 miles, 6 furlongs – at 12 o'clock, having been only two hours. Here Thos. swallowed a little gruel & I was heartily glad when we arrived at Llangollen, ten miles, at about half past three – that he might procure medical advice. He is somewhat better this evening, & I hope – with Mr Rowland's advice & medicine – will be sufficiently recovered – after a days rest – to continue his journey homeward on Monday. Unfortunately the King's Head is so full, that Mr Lloyd cannot take us in, but has procured rooms for us near, & we are waited on by the servant of the Inn. We have one advantage – that of escaping the eternal Welch Harper who never tires, (his hearers excepted), & is seldom bearable.

Augt. 3rd

Thomas sufficiently recovered to resume his journey – we therefore left Llangollen after breakfast and arrived at Shrewsbury to dinner. At Llangollen, therefore, our Tour thro' North Wales came to a conclusion after – upon the whole – a very agreeable excursion. In consequence of Thomas' attack, we saw no more of the vale of Llangollen, the beauty of which is so celebrated, than is to be viewed from the road; but there is I believe, but little more to see; & it is doubtless, very beautiful on both sides of Llangollen – but, as for its rivalling the vale of Festiniog, (a claim which some have been fond enough to advance) the notion is quite preposterous. I walked before evening Church, (the service of which is part in English & part in Welsh – an odd arrangement) to Valle Crucis Abbey, & which just ten years before I visited with my friend Samuel Kent; where I roamed about some time, & was much pleased to renew my acquaintance with that very beautiful & picturesque ruin. The handsome, carved ceiling in Llangollen church, was removed from hence.

Augt. 4th

Slept at Shrewsbury, & drove my poor mare, through Bridgnorth and Stourbridge (a very trying, & today a very hot, road) to Pedmore, where we have now taken up our quarters for a few days; & where we expect fully, to find as civil treatment, as good accommodation, & upon as reasonable terms, as at any house of entertainment at which we have sojourned.

PEDMORE

It is difficult today to recapture the village atmosphere which must have existed in 1835. Pedmore now straddles the

Hagley to Stourbridge road with modern, high quality development. However, the 19th century is to be found by turning off Pedmore Lane to find the church and the Rectory overlooking the village cricket ground.

The old Rectory Pedmore.

But neither the church or the Rectory are as Henry and Thomas would have found them on their return in 1835. The church has been almost completely rebuilt; preserved from the old church are the tower, the south doorway and the repositioned Norman chancel arch. However, in his book, "Old Pedmore and the rebuilding of its church", Geoffrey Parkes records that both Henry and Thomas were present at the consecration of the re-built church in 1871. At about the same time, the Rectory underwent considerable renovation, the present two storey building resulting from the removal of the third floor. Mr Parkes has advised us that before more recent work on the interior, he remembers the remains of a staircase which obviously went to the third floor. The tithe map reproduced in the book shows farm buildings between the rectory and Pedmore Lane, with the entrance of the Rectory opposite the position of the present modern Rectory.

Photograph of a painting of St. Peter's Church, Pedmore, as it was in 1850. (Reprinted by permission of the present Rector.)

No evidence of Philpott graves could be found in the churchyard, but it is probable that the three Rectors lie under the present chancel, as this was extended during the re-building. This assumes that the practice of burying incumbents close to the east window was followed. On the north side of the sanctuary is a memorial tablet to Thomas, the last of the Pedmore Philpotts and his wife Mary.

More About the Philpotts

The Part of the Philpott Family Tree Relevant to Henry Charles

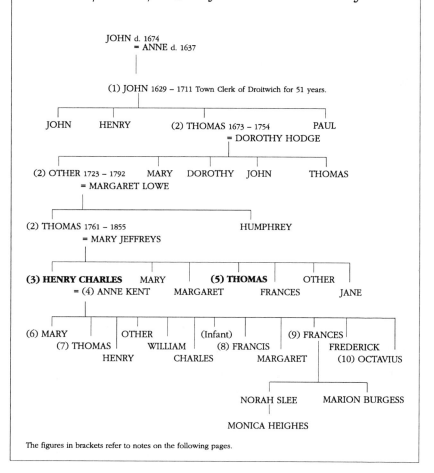

JOHN d. 1674
= ANNE d. 1637

(1) JOHN 1629 – 1711 Town Clerk of Droitwich for 51 years.

JOHN   HENRY   (2) THOMAS 1673 – 1754   PAUL
= DOROTHY HODGE

(2) OTHER 1723 – 1792   MARY   DOROTHY   JOHN   THOMAS
= MARGARET LOWE

(2) THOMAS 1761 – 1855   HUMPHREY
= MARY JEFFREYS

(3) HENRY CHARLES   MARY   **(5) THOMAS**   OTHER
= (4) ANNE KENT   MARGARET   FRANCES   JANE

(6) MARY   OTHER   (Infant)   (9) FRANCES
(7) THOMAS   WILLIAM   (8) FRANCIS   FREDERICK
HENRY   CHARLES   MARGARET   (10) OCTAVIUS

NORAH SLEE   MARION BURGESS

MONICA HEIGHES

The figures in brackets refer to notes on the following pages.

THE PHILPOTT FAMILY

This branch of the Philpott family is very much of Worcestershire. It has been traced back to John Philpott who died in 1674, who is thought to have lived in Blockley which is between Moreton in Marsh and Chipping Campden. This parish, now in the Gloucester diocese, was transferred from Worcester in 1931. It is claimed that this John was a descendant of Sir John Philpott who was Lord Mayor of London in 1378-79.

The family has a great tradition of service in the Church of England. Six generations were clerics, from some time before 1721, when Thomas left Oddingly, (N.W. of Worcester), to go to Pedmore, (between Stourbridge and Hagley), to become the first of three successive generations of Rectors. The sixth generation was John Maxwell Philpott, who died in 1964. All six generations served in the Worcester diocese.

Three of the fourth generation were ordained, Henry Charles, the author of the journal and his brothers, Thomas and Other and four of Henry Charles' sons, Thomas Henry, Francis Octavius (eighth child), Octavius (eighth son) and Charles Humphrey who was ordained in Queensland. To the six generations of Philpotts may be added a seventh generation, H.G. Michael Clarke, a great-grandson of Henry Charles and an eighth generation, Philip, second son of Michael Clarke, in contemporary orders hence spanning over 270 years of ordained ministry to the Church of England.

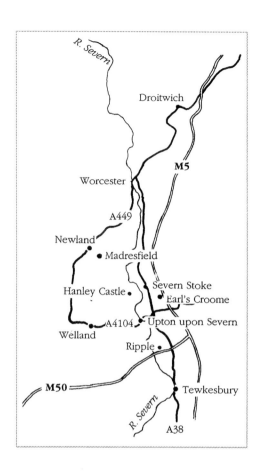

It has been possible to construct a quite extensive family tree, only a part of which is reproduced here, and the following notes are numbered corresponding to the numbers against names in the tree.

1.   JOHN. 1629 – 1711. Town Clerk of Droitwich.

2. The three generations of Pedmore Rectors.

    THOMAS   Rector 1721 – 1754
    OTHER   Rector 1754 – 1791
    THOMAS   Rector 1791 – 1855

The church registers show how tragedy struck the first Thomas and his family in 1726, as the three eldest children all died within a few days of each other. This left Other, then three years old and Mary, then only two. Mary married the Rev'd John Wylde of Belbroughton in 1750. (More about the Wyldes of Belbroughton later)

3. HENRY CHARLES. Author of the journal. Born 16 Feb. 1794 in the parish of St. Nicholas', Worcester, almost certainly at the home of his maternal grandparents, Henry Vaughan and Ann Jeffreys, and died at Earl's Croome Rectory on 21 Oct. 1873. Educated at Rugby and St. John's, Oxford. B.A. 1817, M.A. 1819. Curate of Ripple 1818 – 1825, Curate of Severn Stoke, 1826 – 1855, Rector of Earl's Croome, 1855 – 1873. Married Anne Kent at Earl's Croome.

    The Gentleman's Magazine 1837 Part II p.528 records: Oct. 2nd 1837. At Earl's Croome, The Rev. H.C. Philpott to Anne, third daughter of B.G. Kent Esq. of Levant Lodge.

4. ANNE KENT was born at Hanley Castle in 1812 and lived at Churchend; she died in 1878 and is buried at Earl's Croome with Henry Charles.

Earl's Croome church.

The grave of Henry Charles and Anne Philpott in Earl's Croome churchyard.

She was the daughter of Benjamin Goolden Kent and Anne who at the time of their daughter's marriage to Henry Charles, were living at Levant Lodge, Earl's Croome, which can be seen from the A38 on the Tewkesbury side of Severn Stoke. The Kent family had a cider and vinegar works at Upton on Severn, facing the bridge on a site now occupied by a filling station. According to Mr Finch of Hanley Castle, the company also bottled whisky known as Croome Hunt and the label showed the huntsmen enjoying the product with the hounds being kept waiting outside the door. A copy of the label was provided by Mr Finch. In her book on Upton, published by Phillimore, Pamela Hurle has a photograph of the Kent works.

Littlebury's Directory and Gazetteer of 1879 records:

Kent W & S and Sons (Est. 1778). Importers of foreign wines and spirits and Scotch and Irish Whisky, French wine vinegar, Rectifiers, Impounders and Vinegar makers (prize medal London, 1862). Offices and stores, Church Street, Upton. Bonded stores Gloucester & Bristol.

Henry Charles was obviously well known to the family as he records in his journal that he had visited Valle Crucis Abbey ten years before, 'with my friend Samuel Kent'. The Register of Electors of 1843-44, records Samuel Kent as living at The Hill, Upton.

5.   THOMAS who shared the holiday but not the writing of the journal, was born at Pedmore in 1799. He was at Corpus Christi, Cambridge and gained a B.A. in 1822 and

an M.A. in 1825, ordained Deacon in 1823 and priested in 1824. Curate of Madresfield 1823 – 1857 and Perpetual Curate of Newland 1831 – 1857. The Register of Electors for 1843-44 shows him to be living at the Rectory, Madresfield, which tends to confirm that he had charge of the parish, even though the Rev'd Charles Hill was Rector.

The census of 1861 shows him to be living in Belbroughton with his two unmarried sisters, Mary Anne and Frances, who had presumably remained at Pedmore Rectory until the death of their father in 1855. The choice of Belbroughton must have been influenced by their sister Jane, who was married to the Rev'd. John Wylde, Curate of Belbroughton. Thomas seems to have held no further appointment after 1857 as he is then shown as 'of Belbroughton'. He lived until 1878 and was able to be a member of the rebuilding committee of Pedmore church so it does not appear to have been ill health that caused his retirement to Belbroughton. It may have been a combination of a legacy from his father, the need to provide a home for his sisters and the appointment of a new Rector of Madresfield following the death of Charles Hill, in 1856.

It would appear that Other, who had moved from Clungunford to Welland, had also retired to Belbroughton as he and Thomas are buried in the same grave close to the north east corner of Belbroughton church. Other died in 1861 at the age of 57 so another reason for Thomas going to Belbroughton may have been to help care for his brother.

6. MARY JANE was born on 26 June 1838, the first of the twelve children of Henry and Anne. She married Frederick Kent Clarke, who was a brother of George Row Clarke the architect, painter and illustrator. Frederick was Head Master of King Edward's School, Stafford and later, Rector of Orcheston St. Mary, Devizes. A third brother, Henry James Clarke, emigrated to Melbourne and in 1856, married Mary Elizabeth Kent, born in Hanley Castle in 1824, a sister of Anne. Three daughters of this union, still living in Melbourne in 1919, are remembered in Frederick's will.

    A grandson of Frederick and Mary Jane was H.G. Michael Clarke who became Headmaster of Repton in 1937 and was Provost of Birmingham, 1951.

7. THOMAS HENRY was born on 4 Oct. 1839 and died on 22 May 1917. He married Cecil Ann Bengough of Wotton under Edge, Glos. Among many appointments he was Rector of Stockleigh Pomeroy, Devon, 1894 – 1909.

    Thomas went from Marlborough to Durham University through the generosity of a cousin of his father, a Canon of Durham. It was at the University that Thomas met the Rev'd. J.J. Hornby, which led to the pair pioneering many of the climbs in the Alps between 1861 and 1867. These climbs were recorded by Thomas in a paper published in the Alpine Journal in 1916, 'Hornby and Philpott – Memories of an Alpine partnership in the sixties'. Thomas evidently did not share the view which his father expressed about not climbing Snowdon.

8. FRANCIS OCTAVIUS was born 17 May 1848 and died 25 December 1909. He was Curate at Churchstoke and later, Rector of Little Marcle. His son, John Maxwell Philpott, 1887 – 1964, was the sixth generation Philpott to be ordained into the Church of England.

9. FRANCES was born 10 June 1851 and died 24 February 1944. She married Dr. E.A. Burgess on 25 April 1889 at Knowle, Warwickshire, from the home of her brother, Henry Charles, with another brother, Octavius, officiating. The Journal came into her possession on the death of her mother, Anne. The family moved to the Manchester area at the turn of the century and Frances is buried in Southern Cemetery, Manchester.

10. OCTAVIUS was born 13 Jan. 1854 and died 19 Nov. 1932, the eighth son, twelfth child and the third of his generation to be ordained. Educated at Jesus College, Cambridge, he obtained a B.A. in 1878 and an M.A. in 1881. He was ordained at Salisbury in 1880, was Chaplain to Derby School, 1890 – 1898, Rector of Glenfield, Leics, with Braunston and Kirby Muxloe, 1899 – 1923 and Rector of Kirkby Mallory, 1923 – 1932.

    His brother, Henry Charles, died in 1889 leaving a widow (née Caroline Charlotte Studdy Owen) and eight daughters, who later made their home with the batchelor Octavius at Glenfield Rectory.

Of the remaining children of Henry Charles and Anne, Other, born 12 Aug. 1842, had four sons and two daughters, some of whom emigrated to Winnipeg. William, born 4 March 1844, emigrated to Australia and some of his descendants are still in Western Australia. Charles Humphrey born 4 Sept. 1845, emigrated to Australia before William; the brothers farmed sugar cane for a period at Nerang, Queensland on a property called Biribi and Charles was later ordained to serve the parish of Nerang. Charles had two daughters, Stephana and Constance. Margaret Anne born 26 December 1849, died 27 December 1889 at Pau in the Pyrenees where she had gone for health reasons. Frederick Vaughan, born 12 August, 1852, emigrated to Toronto in 1872 and had two sons and four daughters.

Twice the Philpotts have been linked with another Worcestershire family, the Wyldes. Mary, the daughter of Thomas, the first of the Pedmore Rectors, married the Rev'd John Wylde and their grandson, also John, married Jane, the youngest sister of Henry Charles. The Wyldes served in Belbroughton, just a few miles from Pedmore, but as with Thomas at Madresfield, as Curates, the ministry does not appear to be commemorated. John and Jane also named a son John, born on April 13 1841, who died on St. Stephen's Day 1941. He had been Vicar of St. Savior's, Leeds from 1877 to 1929 and an Honorary Canon of Ripon. He was appointed to the living in Leeds by Dr. Pusey and his obituary records, "He was one of the few remaining links with the first generation of Tractarians" He was educated at Bromsgrove School, Magdelan College, Oxford and prepared for Holy Orders at Cuddesdon, being ordained in 1866. Hence, he must have been at Cuddesdon when Bishop Edward King was Principal.

Of the rest of the generation of Henry and Thomas, the Belbroughton registers show that Mary Anne died in June 1868, John Wylde in March 1873, Frances in November 1882 and Jane Wylde in December 1888. Both Frances and Jane are shown as 'of The Church House', so it would appear that they spent their last years together, as the remaining two of the seven Pedmore brothers and sisters.

FAMILY CORRESPONDENCE

A few letters remain which give an insight into the joys and griefs of Philpott family life after the 1835 holiday.

The earliest are two written at Pedmore to Henry Charles at Severn Stoke and sent together, one from his mother and the other from his sister, Mary Anne. They are written in response to a letter from Henry in which he had sent the news that he was to marry Anne Kent. The letters were written on March 23rd and would have been 1837, although the year is not given.

It would appear from the letter written by his mother, that Henry was looking for another position with a suitable house and a better stipend. However, the problem must have been solved in part by his Rector as the Philpotts stayed at Severn Stoke for the first 18 years of their marriage, during which time, twelve children were born. Adjacent to the church is The Church House, once the Rectory and the inclusion of a photograph in a family album, indicates that this probably was the Philpott home once the new Rectory had been built on the opposite side of the A38. The Rector was the Rev'd T.H. Coventry and the patron was the Earl of Coventry.

Severn Stoke Church.

The Church House, Severn Stoke, the Philpott family home until 1855.

Henry Charles Philpott's
great grand-daughter at The Church House,
Severn Stoke in 1993.
(Photographs of The Church House by permission of
the present owners.)

The letter from Mary Anne sounds excited at the prospect of another family wedding. She advises her brother that he does not need a new suit for the wedding but that his linen should be in good order and offers to get shirts made if he supplies the material and a pattern. It appears that at this time, Mary Anne and her sisters had met Anne Kent, but their mother had not.

The third letter we have is dated August 29th and must have been 1838. It is from Henry's mother to Anne, (by now a mother), in which she thanks Anne for a gift and confirms the arrival of a second grand-daughter, Mary, born that morning to Jane, by then the wife of the Rev'd. John Wylde of Belbroughton. The first grand-daughter was also Mary, (Mary Jane), born earlier that year on 26th June.

There is a letter of five years later from Henry to his sister Margaret, dated September 27th 1843, from which it is learnt that their mother had been unwell, but was now well enough to invite her five year old grand-daughter, Mary Jane, to accompany her father on a visit to Pedmore. The letter gives an insight into the Severn Stoke family activities – a visit from brother Thomas and a dress to be altered, presumably for Mary so that she would be presentable for her grand-parents and aunts at Pedmore.

In this letter, Henry teases his sister about his successful farming and in the same letter is revealed the generosity of their father.

The next two letters are from Henry to his wife who is staying at Pedmore. The first is dated 16th February 1848 and the second, which is undated, was apparently written on the Saturday evening of the same week. Anne was recovering from an illness; some children have been sent to friends or relatives and some, (there were six by this time), are still at home and eating well although they have troublesome coughs.

It would seem that the Severn Stoke source of bread, probably their own kitchen, is better than that at Pedmore, but Henry shows concern that although he wishes to bring the convalescent Anne some bread, he is thoughtful of the feelings of 'Harper', presumably the Pedmore cook. He is also revealed as a caring father; with their mother away, he has his two young sons join him for dinner and the sharing of a treat – a plum pudding. It would be interesting to know what else made it 'a jolly evening'.

Henry records an active social life in which Thomas, still at Madresfield and Other, by now at Welland, (about 4 miles west of Upton), were also involved. Henry is invited for dinner at The Lodge – the home of the in-laws – and at the Rectory. Something of Victorian travel is revealed in the letters, Thomas needs to be collected from Upton and two ladies have left for Bristol from Worcester by the 'Gloucester Rail-road'. Influenza has struck the village and the progress or otherwise of people in the village is related to Anne.

Finally, there is a letter written to Henry by his father from Pedmore. It is dated 27th July 1852 and there is obviously great concern over the health of Margaret. Thomas has been called from Madresfield as he is free from family ties. Henry's father attempts to convey a ray of hope, but he is very concerned and fears the worst, not without cause as Margaret's burial is recorded in the Pedmore registers in 1852.

From the letters the family names are revealed. Henry Charles is known as Harry and Anne is called Nannie by her husband. Of the children, Thomas appears to have remained Thomas, but young Henry is also Harry, William is Willie and Charles is Charlie.

The Revd. Henry Charles Philpott,
M.A.

Anne Philpott (née Kent)

A full postal address on any of the envelopes would have confirmed that The Philpotts had indeed occupied The Church House, but all that was needed by the postal service was:

The Reverend H.C. Philpott,
Severn Stoke,
Worcester.

Neither was it necessary for the writer to put an address at the top of these family letters.

Letter written by Mary Philpott to her son Herny Charles Philpott prior to his marriage to Anne Kent which took place on 2nd October 1837. The letter is dated March 23rd and although no year is given it is likely is was 1837, six months before the marriage.

The Reverend H.C. Philpott,
Severn Stoke,
Worcester.

Many Thanks my ever dear Henry for your truly interesting letter & for your early compliance with my wishes – my earnest prayer is, that the important event which is about to take place may be productive of uninterrupted comfort & enjoyment to you & the deserved object of your affection – if I should live to become acquainted with her I am sure from all I have heard of her I shall love her, not only for yr. sake but her own, & tho' I am now become old, infirm & stupid, I will yet hope to possess some share of her affection if you can spare me any. I like Mr Kent for so justly appreciating yr. worth, & have no doubt you will find in him a kind Father & warm friend, but I am afraid that even his liberality will not prevent yr. being somewhat cramped in yr. circumstances – had I the means to make all things easy how gladly would I bestow it!

I shd. be pleased to hear that you had met with a desirable curacy, but I fear it will be long before you will be able to tell me that you have succeeded in procuring one according to your wishes – I see in the paper many curacies wanted but none sticking on hand.

You will probably have heard before you get this that our old friend Dr. Blakiston is no more – he died at 11 o'clock on Tuesday morning – his poor Wife and Daughters are very unwell in consequence of their loss – & the Wyldes are in a fuss regarding the curacy, which I hope and trust they will be allowed to retain.

I am sorry to tell you that poor Jane has not regained her liberty – she was much better but very imprudently walked in the garden twenty minutes & has ever since been very indifferent – her present indisposition disturbs me much; we had a note from her husband this morning but he cannot boast of her amendment. Fanny was to leave (Ainprot?) for Farnham today – What weather for travelling! Will this winter never end? Mary Anne has desired to employ part of my paper and as William is ready to go to Stourbridge I must conclude in haste with assuring you my beloved son that

I am your truly affectionate Mother

Mary Philpott

Pedmore
March 23rd

Excuse the bad writing of a cold & shaking hand. Let us hear how you are going on.

My dear Harry,

I have begged a portion of my Mother's paper that I may tell you what perhaps you may suppose, that you have my very best wishes that all the happiness you have every reason to expect in your union with Anne Kent may be fully realised. I am not so well acquainted with her as my sisters but from what little I have seen of her and still more from all I hear of her I am fully prepared to find that you have not over-rated her good qualities, and that in her we shall have an affectionate sister. Give my love to her with my sincerest congratulations on her happy prospects. I hope a house and curacy will soon be found, that your happiness may be soon completed. Margaret has just come in and desires that I will say everything that is kind for her.

I believe it is not considered necessary for a gentleman to have wedding clothes but for the wife's sake I think the linen ought to be in a tolerably good state, so if you should wish to have some new shirts and will send me on the cloth and a pattern I will undertake to cut them out and get them made free of expense: neckcloths I could buy at Stourbridge if I knew the size, but it is not a good place for Irish cloth.

I must only add the kindest love of all the party,

Believe me, my dear Harry,
Ever your truly affectionate sister,

Mary Anne Philpott.

p.s. I think my writing requires more apologies than my Mother's but my eyes have not nearly recovered the eriesypelas. [erysipelas]

Letter from Mary Philpott to her daughter-in-law Anne at Severn Stoke, written on 29 August 1838.

Pedmore Rectory Augt. 29th

My dear Anne,

Miss Bufford has kindly given me an opportunity of sending gratis my sincere thanks for your very pretty & sweet Basket which is ingeniously and nicely made & has been much admired here. Your friends will tell you of Mr Philpott's & Margaret's unfortunate accidents; the former I am most thankful to say escaped with only a few bruises which has not caused him a moments confinement but the latter is severely hurt, she fell on her face which is much cut, particularly her nose and her right hand & fingers are so violently bruised & sprained that it is entirely useless & I fear will long continue so – we thought her daily improving ever since the accident till yesterday evening when she was seized with violent pain and heat in her head & appeared very ill & low. Mr Downing saw her last night & again this morning. He thinks her rather better today but says that quietness & keeping her bed is necessary; he means to visit her this evening & I confess that his great attention rather alarms me, tho' he seems to say there is no danger. God grant that it may be so!

I am sure that you & Henry sincerely rejoice with me in the safe arrival of my second grand daughter – Mr Wylde breakfasted with us this morning & appeared a very happy Father – he gives a comfortable account of his Wife &

that my beloved Jane will be a happy Mother of a happy & healthy child. Mary Anne arrived safely at Bristol & found my Brother & Rebecca in good health, the latter accompanied her for a few days to Westbury where I suppose she will enjoy herself for the next fortnight. She gave us good tidings of our friends at Severn Stoke & tells us that my God-daughter tho' small is a very nice child. May she go on thriving to your hearts content!

I have been very unwell lately & am now a poor creature & in an unfit state for writing so you must excuse this very stupid letter – Mr P & Marg't unite with me in kindest love to you, Henry & Mary Jane –

believe my dr. Anne
yr. truly affectionate Mother
Mary Philpott.

Letter dated September 27th 1843 written by Henry Charles Philpott to his sister Margaret about Mary Jane's impending visit to her grandmother. Mary Jane, Henry's daugher, was then 5 years old.

Severn Stoke
Septr. 27th 1843

My Dear Margaret,

I feel pretty sure that more than once, you have exclaimed – 'How very odd it is that Harry takes no notice of my Mother's invitation to Mary'! or some such observation. The truth is we could not decide when I should bring her – First Thomas promised to dine with us one day this week – then there was a frock to be altered and so this week was out of the question – so Tuesday the 3rd of Octr was almost decided upon, when it occurred to us that it would be very ungallant of me to leave my wife all alone on our wedding day, and therefore my journey is put off until Thursday the 5th when I shall be very glad to have a peep at you all and see how my Mother is, and I certainly expect to see her looking better than when I was last at Pedmore or she has no right to be asking a noisy girl to visit her – Mary has just been told of her grand Mamma's kind invitation and she is highly delighted at being allowed to accept it – Rebecca Jeffreys left Madresfield on Monday and with Bessie Herbert proceeded from Worcester by the Gloucester Rail-road for Bristol. This morning a letter arrived for her, which we know not how to forward, and shall therefore send to Madresfield with the hope that Thomas has the proper instructions.

I must not omit to thank my Father for the remainder of my Crouch rents & the addition he was kind enough to send with it – I wish I could put all my money out at such good interest. Not but that I am tolerably successful – You would be surprised at the sums I am realising by my farming – such hay – such calves – such butter! Such abundance of aftermath! but I'll say no more, lest you should think I am getting too rich.

Anne and the scions unite with me in sending our best love to all and believe me dear Margaret,

Yr Affectionate brother,
H.C. Philpott.

[Note: Aftermath – a second mowing of grass in the same season.]

Letter addressed to

Mrs H.C. Philpott,
Pedmore Rectory,
Stourbridge.

Severn Stoke
9 o'clock February 16th 1848

My dearest Anne,

It was a great pleasure to find that you are improving at a quicker rate – you have by this time, I suppose, taken half a dozen turns along the gravel walk. I hope you will not put off your journey till the periodical eastwinds arrive. You of course do not expect to see me before Monday – as it is unreasonable to leave all the Sunday duty to my Rector when there is no necessity for it.

I obeyed your command, and ordered a plum pudding this morning, which I certainly should not have done without it. Having a pudding, it seemed fitting that it should be eaten, so I invited my two sons and we made a jolly evening of it. They are full of engagements this week – Earl's Croome tomorrow – as I told you – and they are to spend Friday evening with Mrs Knott who is "sola". Tomorrow is to be an archery meeting and Mary graciously offers Thomas her Bow on one condition – that he is not to take her favourite arrow. It is hoped it will be a fine day – Willie and Charlie, but especially Willie – are so fat, that you would be quite alarmed lest they should be carried off in a fit of apoplexy! but at present they look uncommonly well. Mrs J.W.M. does not at all like your plan of having all your children here on your return, and hopes you will not insist upon her two coming back until you become accustomed to having a fewer number about you. Stephana also thinks it a bad plan, and wishes to have Harry when Other returns – I have an invite to the Lodge for Friday: I do not know of whom the party is to consist, but there is a request that Mary's white frock and her sash may be sent. O.P. of Welland is to be there: and I learn, in a note this morning from Thomas, that I am to take him up at Upton tomorrow on my way to Madresfield, and to bring him back the next morning for his dinner at the Lodge. What he does with himself on Friday night I have yet to learn. Having made you acquainted with all the sayings and doings I can think of that more immediately concern you, I may be allowed to express my satisfaction that Mary Anne and Fanny are improving. It is really quite time for the latter to bid adieu to her cough. Give my love to them and to my Father and Margaret, and believe me,

Your true husband
H.C. Philpott.

P.S. The Bishop of Worcester was, previously to his translation B.P. of Sodor & Mann

If you think of anything wanted at Worcester, let me know, that I may procure it on Monday – Bye the Bye Mrs Venables, who is considerably better, very kindly hopes that if you feel much tired, you will stop and lie down for an hour at her house.

Once more Adieu.

Letter from Rev. H.C. Philpott to his wife, undated but almost certainly written in February 1848.

My dearest Anne,

I trust fervently that you have continued to advance towards recovery as rapidly as you did the last 12 hours before I left you. Innumerable are the enquiries and congratulations. No sooner did I enter the house yesterday when a note was given me from Mr Dunne to ask me to dine there and meet Mr & Miss Kent & Mrs Broome & Miss Lingen who were all of course highly pleased with my report, and after dinner Mrs Broome proposed a toast – to your perfect recovery. I had scarcely read the note when in came our Rector, hoping to secure me to meet J.L.C. who unfortunately (for I dine at the Rectory tonight) was obliged to leave this morning. With his usual attention, he set his back near my fire for an hour this morning – which, as I find so many things to do that I have no time to shake myself – was very agreeable.

Tomorrow I dine at the Lodge – on Monday with I. Martins. Luckily Mr Grice's note for Tuesday was put into the fire, as your father told him I should not be at home.

The boys have all had the same sort of cough, which has left them with the same sort of piping hoarseness but they all seem pretty well. I made this an excuse to J.W.M. (not their being pretty well – but hoarse) who will take no denial and refers me to his wife who is determined to have them.* Charlie looks uncommonly well and chatters faster than ever. Willie's breath seems more affected than that of the others. I have not seen Mary – Mrs Moss & Miss Clegg have got rid of their influenza. Mr Moss is not considered so well as when you left home: Mr Veneables Snr. died of influenza – he was only ill 4 days, but Mr Carden gave but small hope of his recovery from the first. He was, as you know, very feeble.

As this seems to be a page of enumerations of invalids, I may as well add that yesterday evening was the first yr. father has been out. He seemed pretty well but complains of great difficulty to breathing in the mornings. Since I told Henry Griffin that he must be at Pedmore at ½ past twelve on Tuesday I have had a sort of misgiving whether I mentioned an hour too late. If I have, somebody perhaps will have the kindness to rectify my mistake.

I trust your nurses all keep pretty well and Fanny's 'strict residence' in your room is nearly over. I feel half inclined to bring you a loaf on Wednesday – the bread is so very light. Would Harper be affronted? Oranges I will not forget – they are much cheaper in Worcester. It is nearly 6 o'clock, & I must go & prepare for dinner. My kind love to all & believe me dear Nannie,

Yr. truly affect. husband,
H.C. Philpott

* John Hands appeared with a note from O.P. yesterday evening.

Letter from Thomas Philpott to his son Henry Charles dated July 27th 1852 about the illness of his sister Margaret that was causing the family concern.

July 27th 1852

My dear Harry,

According to my promise I send you an account of your Sister – she had a rough & bad night till 5 o'clock but does not seem to be worse than she was yesterday – indeed if there is any difference Mr Hobbs thinks it is in her favour. Considering that Thomas is more at liberty to leave home than you at present I wrote to him and he is here – If any material change takes place in Margaret you shall hear of it immediately – if not you shall hear again in a few days.

Mary Anne and Thos. Join in kind rememberance to all your circle with

Your affec: Father
Thos. Philpott

N.B. Margaret did not recover and died later that year.

July 27th 1852

My dear Harry

According to my promise I send you an account of your Sister - she had a restless & bad Night till 5 o'Clock but does not seem to be worse than she was Yesterday - indeed if there is any difference Mr. _____ thinks it is in her favour. - Considering that Thomas is more at liberty to leave home than you at present I wrote to him & he is here - If any material change takes place in Margaret - you shall hear of it immediately - if not you shall hear again in a few days

Mary Anne & Thos. join in kind remembrances to all your circle with

your affec: Father

Thos. Philpott

91

Severn Stoke
9 o'clock. Feby 16th
1848

My dearest Anne

It was a great pleasure
to me to find that you are improving
at a quicker rate – You have by this
time, I suppose, taken half a dozen
turns on the gravel walk. I hope you
will not put off your journey till the
periodical east wind arrive. You
of course do not expect to see me before
Monday – as it is unreasonable to
leave all the Sunday duty to my
Rector when there is no necessity for it.
I obeyed your command, & ordered a
plum pudding this morning, which
I certainly should not have done without
it. Having a pudding, it seems fitting
that it should be eaten; so I invited

my two sons, & we made a jolly evening of it. They are full of engage= 2 ments this week – East's broome Tomorrow – as I told you – and they are to spend Friday evening with Mrs Knott who is "Iola." Tomorrow is to be an archery meeting, & Mary graciously offers Thomas her Bow on one condition – that he is not to take her favourite arrow. It is to be hoped it will be a fine day – Willie & Charlie, but especially Willie, are so fat, that you wd be quite alarmed lest they should be carried off in a fit of apoplexy! – but at present they look uncommonly well. Mrs J. W. M. does not at all like your plan of leaving all your children here on your return, & hopes you will not insist upon her two coming back until you are become accustomed to having a fewer number about you. Stephana also thinks it a bad plan, & wishes to have Harry when Other returns — I have an invite to the Lodge for Friday: I do not know who the party is to consist, but there is a request that Mary's white frock & her sash may be sent. O.P. of Welland is to be there: and I learn, in a note this morning from Thomas, that I am to take him up at Upton tomorrow in my way to Madresfield, & to bring him back the next morning for his dinner at L. dodge. What he does with himself on Friday night I have yet to learn. Having now made you acquainted with all the sayings and doings I can think of that more immediately seem to concern you,

94

I may be allowed to express my
satisfaction that Mary Anne & Fanny
are improving. It is really quite time
for the latter to bid adieu to her
cough. Give my love to them & to my
Father & Margaret. I believe me

        Yr true husband
           H.C. Philpott

P.S. The Bishop of Worcester was,
previously to his translation, B.P of
Sodor & Mann. ——

    If you think of anything wanted at
Worcester, let me know that I may
procure it on Monday — By the bye
Mrs Venables, who is considerably better,
very kindly hopes that if you feel
much tired, you will stop & lie down
for an hour at her house.
        Once more Adieu —